EGYPT

EGYPT

Photographs by
DOROTHY BOHM

Foreword by Lawrence Durrell
Text by Ian Jeffrey

With 71 colour photographs

THAMES AND HUDSON

*To my husband Louis
and our daughters Monica and Yvonne*

Typeset in Monophoto Apollo Roman

Printed and bound in Singapore

Contents

Foreword by Lawrence Durrell

It is good news for us all that more of the photographic work of Dorothy Bohm has found a well-merited place between the covers of this book for, in the world of photography, she is a true original and has long been discerned as such and admired by her peers in the art. When one thinks of the reputations of masters like Bill Brandt or Brassaï or Herbert List, to name only three major figures, one cannot help turning an admiring thought in her direction. Her name inevitably strays into the field, an invaluable addition to their ranks; one recalls here the splendid, incisive black-and-whites of city streets in her earlier work. They constitute a sort of commentary on the atmospheres of a number of capital cities – each picture built round the axis of a dramatic situation – an event, a 'scene'. This work, *Egypt*, is full of felicities of observation and intuition, full of artistic slyness, yet it completely avoids showing off. This achievement is so difficult in a field where one is always tempted by the striking, the flashy, when it comes to anecdote or situation. Her pictures sting the aesthetic sense because they are full of an exemplary gravity, full of the poetry of the natural.

In *Egypt* she addresses a single coherent theme and turns all the resources of her lens upon a single subject, a country. One's attention gathers momentum as the pages turn; what prints itself on the mind is a sort of replica of historic time – the whole texture of duration. This patient and humane observer of the human scene has made each exploit of the camera shutter an original and striking commentary on some aspect of the daily life of modern Egypt – these poetic pictures are vignettes full of delicacy and insight – whether the rope merchant squatting in his coils, or the Cairo ironmonger in the Khan el Khalili Bazaar. These are original insights of a fine artist deeply expressive of their theme.

The Nile is huge with history and in its slow, oozing progress seems to summarize and symbolize the fact. In a sense the river is the photographer's Muse, her inspiration.

But Dorothy Bohm had to evolve a camera strategy in order to deal with the distracting and contradictory elements presented by the rich delta, with its variegated anthology of differing and contrasting greens. In this domain her colour work takes on a classical sobriety; it shows profound respect for the desert light in all its hallowed density. Objects – trees, statues, buildings – seem to float in its amber warmth, fixed in a trance-like haze, as if they were the creations of Memory itself – the old desert sandstones and marbles surrendered by the wind of history. Her landscapes swim or rather float in this dense, honeyed light, transformed into dramatic pictorial ikons coaxed into being by the attention of her observant camera. Such work is the fruit of a profoundly observant sensibility and a gift of introspection.

It is not every photographer who can follow the print through every stage of its developments until the final production, but Dorothy Bohm has always been rather proud that, as a student in Manchester, she became fully versed in the technology of the darkroom and the full control of her product down to the last printing and framing. It was in 1946 that she raised the capital to found the innovative Studio Alexander in Manchester. In the meantime, her qualities as a lecturer and *animatrice* had brought her to the notice of the Ministry of Information and she gained a valuable link with officialdom as an interpreter of political briefs in the war against Hitler. This fortuitous link with the ministry and the press corps also brought her precious new contacts, giving her an increased sophistication of outlook to match her technical know-how. On the technical side the age had formed itself around the invention of film of differing speeds; the reign of the old plate cameras was over. Though they were robust and sensitive, the hampering weight of the old cameras had been an encumbrance. These new inventions promised mobility and versatility, precious additions for the photographer in the field.

It would be difficult to overestimate the part played by these new cameras in the evolution of the photographic criteria, particularly in the world of the press. I am thinking of inventions like the Rolleiflex Reflex Camera with the old Tessar lens. In my professional career as a press attaché I was able to evaluate the importance of such superb equipment and I have encountered a number of skilled photographers whose professional reputation has been won thanks to such splendid instruments. Dorothy Bohm found her feet during this exciting if somewhat muddled period, encouraged by friendships with painters and sculptors who appreciated her photography, and she made full use of her possibilities, greeted by a steadily expanding professional reputation which flowered in such books as *A World Observed* (1970). In 1980 the BBC treated her to a full-scale television documentary and she published three more texts with illustrations. It was as if at last her art had matured and evolved into full competence. We can take as proof positive these splendidly opulent studies of Egypt – the Egypt of everyday, yet at the same time a very personal Egypt, the private Egypt of the artist, unique and full of colour and sap. There is little doubt that such fine polished creations are destined to stay. Dorothy Bohm belongs to the future.

LAWRENCE DURRELL

Alexandria's Eastern Harbour.

A coffee house in Alexandria.

Alexandrian street scene.

11

Entrance to the Abu el Abbas Mosque in Alexandria.

After winter rain,
Alexandria.

Fishermen sorting their catch, Rosetta.

Boat-builder's yard, Rosetta.

26 July Bridge, Cairo.

Food vendor's trolley in the Khan el Khalili Bazaar, Cairo.

Selling newspapers in Cairo.

Cairo market scene.

Cairo rope merchant.

In the Khan el Khalili
Bazaar, Cairo: an
ironmonger.

Fashion in the Khan el
Khalili Bazaar, Cairo.

A hatter's in the Khan el
Khalili Bazaar, Cairo.

Game of chess in a Cairo suburb.

The street colours of Cairo.

Remains of a cinema poster on a Cairo wall.

The spiral minaret at the
Ibn Tulun Mosque, Cairo.

The courtyard fountain of the Sultan Hassan Mosque, Cairo.

The City of the Dead: the burial garden of the Mameluk
sultans, Cairo.

School children on a Friday outing at the Chephren Pyramid, Giza.

Dusk at Sakkara: the entrance to the pyramids and ancient city ruins.

The Cheops Pyramid, Giza,
from the Mena House Hotel.

33

Early winter morning at the pyramids, Giza.

House with painted wall commemorating the owner's pilgrimage
to Mecca, Oasis of Fayoum.

Hand-prints to ward off the evil eye on a house wall, Memphis.

Evening on Lake Karun,
Oasis of Fayoum.

Water-bearers at Fayoum.

On the shores of Lake Karun, Oasis of Fayoum.

The old village of Dendera.

Farmhouse on the west bank of the Nile, Thebes.

The Temple of Karnak.

Obelisk, Temple of Karnak.

The west bank of the Nile at Thebes.

Donkey water cart outside
Theban house decorated to
record the owner's
pilgrimage to Mecca.

Farmstead with the Theban Hills in the background.

Barren landscape at Thebes on the way to the Valley of the Kings.

Sunset on the Upper Nile.

The Theban bank of the Nile,
opposite Luxor.

Ferry crossing to the west bank from Luxor.

The Nile and the Theban Hills at sunset.

Midday street scene
in Luxor.

Wall graffiti in Luxor.

Morning cleaning outside the temple colonnade of Amenophis III, Luxor.

Sunset at the temple
ruins, Luxor.

The temple of Amenophis III, Luxor.

Low relief on the temple at Philae.

The courtyards of the temple at Philae.

Overleaf l. to r.
An Aswan greengrocer.
An Aswan tailor.
Nubian village women shopping
in the Aswan market.

Billboards at Aswan.

Camels for hire in the desert below the Aga Khan
Mausoleum, Aswan.

Nile tourist boat moored outside Aswan.

Granite outcrops in the Upper Nile cataract region.

Sunset from the Old Cataract Hotel, Aswan.

Boy with a toy felucca on
the Nile, Aswan.

A pavement café in February, Aswan.

Friday at the mosque in Aswan.

Nubian landscape and village near the First Cataract.

The courtyard of the Temple
of Horus, Edfu.

The forecourt of the Ptolemaic temple at Kom Ombo on the Upper Nile.

The Great Temple of Ramses II at Abu Simbel.

A chamber in the Great
Temple, Abu Simbel.

Frieze at the entrance to the Great Temple, Abu Simbel.

Sehel, a Nubian village.

Entrance to a village house, Sehel.

Outside the temples of Abu Simbel.

Houses in a Nubian village.

Egypt Observed by Ian Jeffrey

Egyptian art always meant more than the mere ebb and flow of Egyptian history as told in the guide books. It meant something to European photographers in the 1920s, for example, when the grave, hieratic style of Egyptian statuary served as a model for new objective portraits which stressed physical presence. Artists in the 1920s were worried by the idea of an automated present leading to a completely schematized future, and in the face of that threat Egyptian art was a reminder of presence and of identity.

The hieratic style served its turn, but Europe was haunted afresh, by dreams of barbarism and alienation, of societies out of touch with this place and with its ambience. These photographs by Dorothy Bohm reflect on ambience, and insist on integration, on an accord between humanity, its places and its past. They are, of course, of 'everyday life' along the Nile, but it is a life which has been seen via Chephren, Ti, Rahotep, Nofret, and those other dynastic names who walk the museum cases of the world.

In these photographs the dynastic names and their attendants can be seen on the river's edge, or standing, walking, turning in the street. That is one sort of connection between now and then, but it is not what distinguishes these pictures. There are parallels, but there is also a coherency established by colour. Whether in flesh or in stone, Dorothy Bohm's Egyptian ideals move in their idyll among continuities given in colour, often in the blues of water, sky, shadow and costume. Sometimes that sense of an ensemble threaded together from closely related tones is disrupted by, for example, vivid greens and oranges on palm trees which might have ornamented a set for *Aida*, but these brisk dramatic elements only disclose, by their difference, the integrated beauty of the rest.

The photographs suggest, or make up, something like a natural Egypt, interwoven from the given colours of the place and the gestures of its people. At the same time the photographer returns often, and spectacularly, to artifice, or to make-up. In one of the most striking pictures here an outline or stencil of an ancient head ornaments a sprayed and daubed wall beyond the bare frame of a

chair. Her Egypt is also a store-house and a studio, from which something extravagant will be put together: those striped and ornamented dresses in the window, and all those glittering veils.

Bohm's Egypt amounts to much more than another picture of Egypt just going about its business – although it is that too. It is, like every Egypt represented by a European artist or writer, an imagined land. It looks, if anything, like the place once described by Pierre Loti, although he was outspokenly preoccupied by sham and by the impact of development on the fabric of an ancient culture. Loti was intrigued by the balletic side to Egyptian work, by those ritualized movements celebrated here. Dorothy Bohm is the latest in a line of 'Egyptian' commentators and visionaries, dreamers about right order or harmony. I propose to look at some of the outstanding figures in that tradition.

Visitors to Egypt have had to contend with, among many other things, texts purporting to be authoritative texts. The place had been written about like nowhere else and was becoming, by the 1840s at least, a paradise for pedants. There would be starred guide-books to the historic sites of Ancient Egypt ('Those confounded stars!' Julius Meier-Graefe, bemoaning the Baedeker influence in 1931) and, in addition, there was Edward William Lane's five hundred pages and more of *An Account of the Manners and Customs of The Modern Egyptians*, written in Egypt during 1833–35, partly from notes compiled there between 1825 and 1828. The book was first published in 1836, and its fifth edition came out in 1860. Lane's scrupulous and exhaustive account of Egyptian society told enough inside stories and offered enough insights to satisfy generations of readers. His successors found *The Modern Egyptians* indispensable, and it shapes most accounts of nineteenth-century Egypt. Writers either borrowed from it wholesale, used it in appendices to supplement their more personal and impressionistic accounts, or took it as an excuse to overlook Egyptian society altogether. Gustave Flaubert, for example, who was in Egypt between November 1849 and June 1850, where he was known as Abu-Chanab or 'Father of the Moustache', told his mother in a letter to consult Lane's book for details of the place.

Lane was encyclopedic and full of secrets, and anyone who had read him would have felt familiar with the inside of Egyptian, in particular Cairo, society. How were Cairo houses safeguarded, for instance? Lane gives two paragraphs

with diagrams of wooden locks. On the materials and patterns used in tattooing, he expands over several pages. He recounts intricate jokes. Why, for instance, is a saint or 'welee' also an idiot or 'beleed'? Because the numerical value of the letters composing the words add up in both cases to 46. And on Egyptian food he was never less than appetizing; on 'fetteh', for example, a mutton dish prepared for the Great Festival of El-'Eed el-Kebeer, in which the meat is 'cut into small pieces, placed upon broken bread, upon which is poured the broth of the meat, and some vinegar flavoured with a little garlic fried in a small quantity of melted butter, and then sprinkled over with a little pepper'.

Lane's Egypt, despite mosquitoes, vermin infestations and an outbreak of plague in 1835 which carried off eighty thousand people (one third of the population of Cairo), lay next door to paradise. He could be censorious, although not for long, and he regretted Arab addiction to tobacco which led them 'to waste, over the pipe, many hours which might be profitably employed'. On the other hand, addiction to tobacco superseded 'in great measure, the use of wine, which, to say the least, is very injurious to the health of the inhabitants of hot climates'. Lane doted on ceremonial, ritual, or even mere routine, and his account is rich in descriptions of smoking, eating and the drinking of coffee. His society valued propriety and correct procedures, not because it was controlled by martinets, but because the Egyptian system allowed for interval, and in that interval luxuriance might be savoured. His sixteenth chapter, on 'The Bath', is devoted to 'one of the greatest luxuries enjoyed by the people of Egypt', and in it the writer is specific about towels, sponges, the temperature of water, the cracking of joints, the textures of foot rasps, and the pleasures of massage followed by coffee and tobacco. The coffee might have been flavoured with cardamom-seed ('habb-han') or ambergris ('ambar'), and the tobacco might have been 'mountain tobacco' from El-Ladikeeyeh, in Syria. The bather might then have returned to a house scented with frankincense ('bakhoor el-barr') burnt in charcoal in a chafing-dish. In three luxuriant chapters on 'Domestic Life' he evokes a world rich in gilded sherbet-cups, embroidered silk, waxed cloth lanterns and almost everything else which might have come to the hand of better-off Egyptians enjoying the intervals in their daily routines.

Pipes, and coffee, and sherbet were part of the attraction, a necessary part of the Egyptian paradise, but Lane's Egypt catered for far more than the senses.

Flaubert remarked (in a letter of 5 January 1850 to his mother) on the extravagance of language in Cairo. Maxime du Camp, his photographer travelling companion, had asked a groom if he wasn't tired, and the answer had been: 'The pleasure of being seen by you suffices.' Flaubert, who was also noting recipes and listing perfumes in the style of Lane, was on the way to discovering Egypt's secret, a secret everywhere declared by Lane: that Egypt was the Land of the Word. For example, in 'Character', Lane has a true believer object to the branding of government camels with the name of the then ruler of Egypt, Mohammad 'Alee, for they were also the names of the Prophet and of his Cousin, and the job entailed their names going into the fire and then certain pollution by impure blood. Lane's modern Egyptians lived in a wonderland, a world liable to be turned upside down by a phrase, an original land of Cockaigne. The book itself, with its wealth of sections, sub-sections, anecdotes, footnotes and illustrations expressed an image of a culture which could be savoured or undergone but certainly never seen in its entirety. Lane made doubly sure that no concept of Egypt would get the upper hand for he insisted throughout on phonetics; his *Modern Egyptians* is one of the noisiest of books, insistently accented.

There were absolutes to be identified among a pious people, and in 'Character' he quoted a school prayer which asked God to 'destroy the infidels . . make their children orphans and defile their abodes . . . . .'. The prayer intensified, but at the same time Lane noted that the Muslims of Egypt were 'as remarkable for their toleration as for their contempt of unbelievers'. The next sentence makes a close and paradoxical connection between the religious impulse and 'hypocrisy and pharisaical ostentation'. The name of God, so respected, was frequently invoked in even the most indecent songs. Famous phrases from the Qur'ān were often quoted in jest and in dubious wordplay. And many of the butchers in Cairo were, at least in the 1820s, Jewish. Of course, there had been complaints to the authorities about this Jewish butchering for a Muslim clientele. However, God had commanded, 'Eat of that whereon the name of God hath been commemorated.' The Jewish slaughterers admitted to repeating before the act, 'In the name of God. God is most great', and that settled the legitimacy of their work in the eyes of the authorities. Lane, in these and in many other incidents throughout his tapestry, was celebrating, even revelling in, a culture which admitted to a preternatural power in words, invented less for any metaphysical role than for the delight of humankind – and as a *cordon sanitaire* between a more or less sybaritic Man and a God prone to intransigence.

The modern Egyptians lived in inconsistency, in a world where 'constant veracity' was 'a virtue extremely rare', and where just as simpletons might be saints, as joke 46 put it, so beggars might be wealthy. Lane began his account of begging in a most governmental manner: 'A very great number of persons of both sexes among the lower orders in Cairo, and in many other towns in Egypt, obtain their subsistence by begging.' But there was, as ever, more to it than met the eye for, despite their rags, some of Cairo's beggars had accumulated small fortunes, and one story of inter-beggar theft involved pots of gold coin. The section ends with an account of a dervish beggar processing on horseback through Nile villages preceded by two flag-bearers and a drummer. Lane's own principal informant, recounted in a long description in the preface, signals the extraordinary at source, for he is a nearly blind bookseller (remarkable in itself) who is also a member of an order of dervishes 'particularly famous for devouring live serpents'. Moreover, the informant, Sheyk Ahmed, had been disciplined by his order for repeated glass-eating during religious frenzies. Glass-eating was not within the Saadeyeh order's list of permitted miracles, and seems to have been a stunt normally associated with unattached lunatic saints, elsewhere regarded by Lane as either idiots or impostors: 'Some of them eat straw, or a mixture of chopped straw and broken glass; and attract observation by a variety of absurd actions.' Nevertheless, he emphasized from the outset that an insistent glass-eater was one of his prime informants. It was one way of ruling out the action of normal, or at least European, standards from the outset.

Gérard de Nerval, who spent much of 1843 in Cairo, presented himself as a gauche traveller in his *Voyage en Orient* which first appeared in the *Revue des Deux Mondes* in 1846 and 1847. He would eventually be admired among the Surrealists for walking in the garden of the Palais Royal with a lobster on a leash of blue ribbon, and was never a simple citizen. However, in Egypt he began as a plain traveller keen to see the sights and to take in something of the life of the place while adhering to local rules. His deference had unexpected consequences. He would take a house for six months to avoid the isolation of hotel life, but that, he found, entailed marriage. He took advice, which was either casual or simple-minded, and set out to follow two women muffled in black silk and green levantine; they turned out to be Frenchwomen of good family.

More advice brought him a range of children on approval, some already married and divorced, and for some he was expected to pay the parents heavily. Beautiful male dancing girls cropped up ('khowals' – a cut above the Armenian, Jewish, Greek and Turkish 'ginks', described by Lane). Finally his dragoman and the French consul advised him to buy a slave. He began by terrifying a group of Nubians who mistook his gloves for removable skin and thought him of the devil. Then, got up in local costume and with his head shaven, he bought a Javanese from a caravan recently come in from Mecca. He had seen her like in Dutch paintings. The beautiful Javanese pointed out to her owner that she was a 'cadine' (lady) and not an 'odaleuk' (servant). Determined to make the best of things, de Nerval began to learn Arabic, aided by the lady slave. That too turned out oddly, for the writer learned imperfectly, and one upshot was that the captain of the boat taking de Nerval and entourage to the coast of Palestine offered to exchange his cabin boy for the beautiful Javanese. The writer, one morning, had found the cabin boy washing his face in scarce drinking water and meaning to refer to him as a little rascal used the term 'ya kabibe', a term which had been translated for him by an Armenian only slightly less ignorant than himself. In its song source, and elsewhere, it meant 'little darling'.

De Nerval found bathos everywhere. Having been propelled up the Great Pyramid at top speed by four Arab porters, he held back from describing the already well-known view. What caught his eye was that every Englishman who had made the climb had carved his name on the stone, and some had added their addresses. A blacking merchant of Piccadilly had described his invention, mentioning an 'improved patent'. At the outset de Nerval's Arab dragoman, or interpreter, refused to share the same hotel, as socially demeaning; the dragoman had originally been on the lookout for an Englishman, a higher class of client.

In a typical piece of interpretation de Nerval accounted for the topknot left by his new Turkish barber as stemming from the Turkish abhorrence at the possibility of being picked up by nose or ear in the case of beheading. (He also mentioned a more decorous explanation featuring the hand of God and an elevation into heaven.) De Nerval was engrossed by downbeat, and often eccentric, readings of myth. He told a story, at length, in which the pyramids were built by a King Saurid as giant air-raid shelters in response to a dream in which the stars oppressed the earth. A Prussian officer told him in detail about the initiation rites of the Ancient Egyptians, and added that Moses had failed the demanding course, and had led his people from Egypt largely out of pique. Orpheus and Pythagoras also failed, and as a consequence established their own sects. De Nerval also noted that the mosque of the caliph Hakem, founder of the Druses and 'the last revealer . . . . . the last god whom the world has produced, who still has believers more or less numerous', was in ruins and used by ropemakers.

De Nerval described his Prussian explanations as Voltairean. Flaubert, too, invoked Voltaire in a letter to Louis Bouilhet on 13 March 1850. At Sheik Sa'id, at the tomb of a Moslem saint, birds were supposed to drop food for the consumption of travellers. No one who had read Voltaire would believe this kind of thing, Flaubert added. Flaubert was coarse where de Nerval was disenchanted. In the same letter to his Rouen friend, Bouilhet, Flaubert told a grotesque story of Coptic monks crying for 'baksheesh' in the Nile around his boat and being insulted and treated to obscene displays by the crew. In an earlier letter to Bouilhet (1 December 1849) he wrote with pleasure of the grotesque as an unexpected element in Cairo: 'All the old comic business of the cudgelled slave, of the coarse trafficker in women, of the thieving merchant — it's all very fresh here, very genuine and charming.' Flaubert, too, climbed the Great Pyramid (Cheops) with difficulty, and his friend, the photographer Maxime du Camp, almost died of breathlessness. He took longer over the view than de Nerval, and noted different graffiti: a business card for 'Humbert, Frotteur', and in black letters the name of Buffard, 79 rue Saint-Martin, wallpaper manufacturer. Jenny Lind was commemorated by an English admirer, and Louis-Philippe was there too, as a pear. But Flaubert's graffitists were imbeciles. Wildlife also played its irreverent part, as Flaubert noted in Thebes where, for once, he admitted to being impressed by the ruins: 'Birdshit is Nature's protest in Egypt; she decorates monuments with it instead of with lichen and moss.' Theology and history seemed to interest him hardly at all, even less than his official mission which was to collect information which might interest Chambers of Commerce. In Cairo, Flaubert stayed at the Hotel du Nil, run by Bouvaret and Brochier.

Florence Nightingale also wrote her first letter from Egypt in November 1849. She stayed until April, and wrote at far greater length than Flaubert, who remained until July. At twenty-nine, she was a year older than Flaubert and a more dutiful (and amusing) writer. She saw the pyramids in critical, Victorian, commercial terms: 'Hardly anything can be imagined more vulgar, more uninteresting than a Pyramid in itself, set upon a tray, like a clipt yew in a public-house garden; it represents no idea; it appeals to no feeling; it tries to call forth no part of you, but the vulgarest part – astonishment at its size – at the expense.' On and in the the pyramids in March she wrote of herself as a rat who ought to have been a mole. She enjoyed a feud among pet chameleons on her Nile boat.

She was well-read, in the Bible, Milton and Herodotus, and went with a mind made up; within a few days of landing in Alexandria she felt able to give an assessment of government failings in Egypt, and to compare the Bedouin favourably to the Arab. She was most moved, though, by Egypt as a holy or at least legendary land. She was constantly returned to origins, and to the stories of her childhood, less by inscriptions and relics than by events and by natural phenomena.

Egypt licenced her to write like an Old Testament prophet, or as a later British poet in that guise. She was mightily impressed, for instance, by an ascent of the Cataracts by boat. She felt herself involved in 'as grand an epic poem as any I ever read in Homer or Milton'. She wrote of the boatmen as epic heroes: '. . . in Egypt the wild Nubian rides on the wave, and treads upon the foam'. He is like Cowper's God in the Olney Hymns who 'plants his footsteps in the sea,/And rides upon the storm'. At Karnak, on the last night of 1849, she was Isaiah in front of what looked 'like a mountain fallen to ruin, not a temple. How art thou fallen from heaven, oh Lucifer son of the morning!' Her first encounter with the desert gave her the tongue of Christ speaking for Matthew on the Mount of Olives: 'It is not the desolation: there may be the *solitude* of desolation; but this is the *abomination* of desolation.' She admitted, on 9 December, that there were no words to describe an African sunset, yet in the next sentence she brought up 'a pillar of fire', and Moses in the Desert. The colours of Africa, she continued, were those of precious stones, 'the colours of the Revelations'. By contrast, the colours of Europe were like flowers. Clearly she relished the colours of Africa, although the reference to Revelations endangers her position somewhat. The most colourful character in that book was the Whore of Babylon seated on a scarlet coloured beast, and the city specialized in purple, scarlet and gold. The new Jerusalem in the new heaven was more arcanely and tastefully decorated.

Moreover, Old Cairo, to the south of the city, had been on the site of the ancient Babylon of Egypt, where Moses met Pharaoh, and whence Peter sent his First Epistle.

Her Egypt was at once Paradise and Hell. There were radical differences between the thronged city and the desert as an *abomination* of desolation. Thebes, near to the Valley of the Kings in Upper Egypt, appeared beautiful and biblical after 'the extreme ugliness of Egypt'. She never felt far from the aura of death: Thebes looked to her like the death of a *world*, and she described travelling in Egypt as the activity of a 'ghoul haunting the tombs'. She added, however, that the real ghoul (a word from the Arabic) was Richard Lepsius, 'rifling, and despoiling the monuments, stealing the bodies'. Lepsius was a great German Egyptologist who had headed a Prussian expedition to Egypt and Nubia in 1842–45.

The captain, or 'reis', of her boat on the journey south reminded her of a Rembrandt. At Elephantine Island, near to Aswan, the islanders looked like the products of the cauldron in *Macbeth*, and the crew in rain at Manfaloot seemed to be thinking on the Day of Judgement. Sailing south from Cairo she looked back and saw 'a bright line of yellow bordering the Nile, barley or lupins, the hard brown of the desert behind, a white ghastly Cairo in the background, dabs of Prussian-blue-and-gamboge trees stuck about. It looked as if a child had painted it, and did not know how, and had made it unlike nature.' She began that vision, 'I cannot describe', and the child artist was at a loss too. Egypt was impossible, in other words, which seems to have meant that she was free to write unconstrained, drawing on a wealth of eschatological reading, and bizarre and affecting memory. Her Egypt is a literary apocalypse, a re-telling of the Bible in a setting where normal prose was out of the question. Although accompanied by Charles and Selina Bracebridge, who would go with her to the Crimea, Florence Nightingale wrote as if set apart by the fierce colouring and sonority of her imagination. She lived with the prophets, with Moses confronting Pharaoh and with Ezekiel and his vision of the dry bones, whereas most of her contemporaries and all of her successors made do with passing traffic, and in particular with other travellers such as themselves – odder, certainly, than anything Ezekiel had to offer.

Egypt became a stage, less for Macbeth's Weird Sisters than for travelling personnel from the *Charivari* lithographs Flaubert remarked in the Hôtel du Nil.

The greatest of all these entertainers were the English, a race apart, and as arcane as anything offered by Pharaonic Egypt. De Nerval's Englishmen never spoke without being introduced, and he imagined the embarrassment of meeting one at the summit of a pyramid. His ideal rode a donkey, wore a white mattress hat, a green veil against the dust, and an indiarubber coat with an outer covering of waxed linen to safeguard him against the plague and chance contacts with passers-by. Two pairs of goggles, framed in blue steel, kept out the dazzle of the sun. Flaubert, on hands and knees, passed the time of day with an English party crawling through the Great Pyramid, but he was never a caricaturist. De Nerval's grotesque was a solitary, but during the 1860s they began to come in hordes, under the aegis of Thomas Cook who began his tours after a successful visit by the Prince and Princess of Wales in 1862. By the 1870s tourism was part of the Egyptian experience, with its own distinct social and national hierarchies.

In Amelia B. Edwards' *A Thousand Miles Up The Nile*, published in 1877, one of the first things noticed is the difference between a Cook's tourist and an independent traveller, and the independents were distinguished in their turn between those who were bound for the First Cataract and those who meant to get to the Second, those who had booked a Nile boat (a 'dahabeeyah' here) only for the trip and those who had booked for a month. A French writer and illustrator, Georges Montbard, delighted in such differences in his book of 1894, *The Land of the Sphinx*. On board the steamer *Said*, Marseilles to Alexandria, there were living parcels forwarded by Thomas Cook and Son and unlabelled Englishmen who 'sought insidiously to widen the distance between themselves and the former, while these, like consummate strategists, exerted themselves none the less insidiously to diminish it. The struggle was silent, stubborn, incessant.' Montbard's English were prudent time-keepers, and as 'packages', offset the vigorous French trio who were his heroes.

Montbard's tourists, although they travelled in groups and collected souvenirs, were harmless foils, not to be compared to an omniscient German specialist, Dr. Reptilius (perhaps from an anagrammatic memory of the Egyptologist Richard Lepsius, decried by Nightingale). *The Land of the Sphinx*, though full of lore and observation and vivaciously illustrated, had France as its true subject. The German savant spoke confidentially to an Italian, and the French then declaimed on the threat to their liberty. The defeat at Sedan came up, and 'a flabby Caesar' and betrayal, and the promise of a fatal duel in which one nation would finally perish. Montbard's three constituted the Spirit of France: Jacques, an artist and man of good sense, held the middle ground; Onésime Coquillard, a comic patriot from the boulevards, stood for the irrepressible spirit of France; and Doctor Alan Kéradec, an all-purpose savant and 'Breton bretonnant', embodied autochthonous wisdom. Onésime, a *bon viveur* and ladies' man, rode dangerously on an ass called 'Monsieur de Lesseps' (for the Suez Canal had been open in '69), fell asleep in the mosque of Mahomet Ali and believed in Progress, and in its comforts. Onésime, as a sceptical man of the people, asked questions of the learned doctor, who in his turn was able to appear as witty, charming and a man of parts. In contrast to this company the Germans appeared as fanatics and the English as automata.

Tourism, which had been a comic matter in the 1880s when Montbard was writing, took on darker tones for Pierre Loti in his *Egypt*. Loti was affronted by the tinsel of modern times, and by vulgarity, by hotel orchestras, electric lighting and bridge parties. Baedeker and Cook were his demons, with Cook and his English clients singled out: Thomas Cook & Son (Egypt Ltd.), '. . . the veritable sovereigns of modern Egypt'. The Cooks and Cookesses were at their worst enjoying luncheon in the temple of Osiris at Abydos, just to the north of Thebes: 'They wear cork helmets, and the classic green spectacles; drink whisky and soda, and eat voraciously sandwiches and other viands out of greasy paper, which now litters the floor.' Worst of all, they talked as loudly as he had heard cigar-smokers talking in the shadow of the Sphinx. And there was also the merciless whistling of the railway running parallel to the Nile, and the intolerable groaning and vibration of dynamos on the tourist boats, three-storeyed barracks in Loti's scheme of things.

The tourists marched in battalions to the noise of dynamos, and were only to be deflected by the sound of lunch bells. Loti was saddened by Luxor, with its colossal Winter Palace Hotel, 'obviously sham, made of plaster and mud, on a framework of iron', and angered by the barrage at Aswan. Not only had the barrage submerged the Isle of Philae, with its Temple of Isis, which was accounted one of the marvels of the world, but development (metamorphosis was Loti's term) had brought hairdressers and bars, and a dining room in the Cataract Hotel modelled on a mosque in Stamboul. Aswan, as the end of the tourist-boat line, was also the noisiest port on the river.

Tourism stood for vulgarity and sham. From Loti's point of view European culture was on a downward track, almost lost in a labyrinth of fakery, distracted by hotel orchestras, alcohol and last year's frippery. Egypt allowed him to identify the malaise, because alternatives could still be recognized there especially at El-Azhar, 'the most renowned Moslem university in the world'. He admired the place itself, the serenity of its courtyard and arcades, and was captivated by chanted reading from the book of the Prophet. He recognized, in the voice of gold intoning in the mosque, an elegy 'of the universal death of faith in the heart of man'. He was touched by the archaic simplicity of Coptic ritual, and in front of the ruins of Ancient Egypt could readily imagine 'all the sublime, fresh-minded striving of the human soul after the Unknowable' (words for Thebes). Egyptian labour, especially irrigation by 'shaduf', he described in musical, balletic terms; it was the kind of structured, traditional activity which gainsaid everything that was meretricious in the new occidental Egypt of hotels and factory chimneys, 'impudently high, that disfigure everything, and spout forth into the twilight thick clouds of black smoke'.

In *An Egyptian Journal* of 1985 William Golding made similar remarks, though restrainedly, about brickworks which he noticed everywhere on the Nile banks. Loti in Egypt was nothing less than an Early Modern, discontented with surface effects which obscured a world of such essences as he intuited in that chanting at El-Azhar and among the ruins by moonlight – he went out after hours whenever possible, and began his *Egypt* at night in front of the Sphinx.

Egypt was a site on which Europe's destiny might be imagined. Loti was in no doubt about either degeneration or redemption. The German art historian Julius Meier-Graefe was subtlety personified in his Egyptian journey of 1931, *Pyramid and Temple*, but Europe was his subject too. Meier-Graefe, one of the great interpreters of Cézanne, travelled with Babuschka who boiled over inside in an early conversation with other German tourists, one of whom, from Krostewitz, near Leipzig, maintained that there was something fundamentally Jewish in the Egyptian atmosphere, and that she couldn't abide it. Meier-Graefe's Egypt was ominous. There was something in the air which alerted him to such portents as the black iron crane which controlled the sluices on the Aswan barrage. Looking like a gallows and driven by a small black man with a grey beard, the crane haunted Meier-Graefe as he travelled on the flooded valley to Philae (much overestimated by Baedeker, he thought). At first the crane meant absentee (English) business, capable of any enormity which would serve its turn, but came in the end to signify some unspecified future horror. Memories of the crane came back when they returned after a three-month journey into Nubia to find that the Sphinx had been patched up with reinforced concrete. Meier-Graefe, an authoritative and persuasive judge of art, knew that the Great Sphinx was one of the noblest works of mankind, and he had seen it treated with contempt by a restorer he described as an ex-railway employee, authorized by a director-general of Egyptian antiquities who was a philologist. Meier-Graefe loathed specialists of all nations, and especially German and English Egyptologists, because in every case knowledge had ousted judgement.

His account of Egyptian art is unequalled, because he was preoccupied by worth and by a feeling that his own age was adrift, taking snapshots indiscriminately (as he put it). The art of the Old Kingdom was the greatest art the world had ever seen, and in that age King Chephren, sponsor of the Great Sphinx and of the central pyramid at Giza, was paramount. Afterwards there was a long decline. He had no formula, and seems to have admired the often severe, conventionalized work of the Old Kingdom on humanist grounds; it was an art which was at once natural and complete. Trying to find adequate terms he invoked Cézanne, whom he described as building his own pyramids near to Aix, and Corot, whose 'spontaneous persuasiveness' came to mind in front of sculpted family groups in the Cairo Museum. His ideal art was at once systematic and sympathetic, and unrealizable this side of utopia. The Tutankhamen treasures, unearthed in 1922, were, Meier-Graefe thought, fit only for a darkened room or export to the Argentine.

The despised English had their own visions of Egypt, although they were never prompted by premonitions of the end of civilization. E.M. Forster's *Alexandria*, which was published in that city in 1922, looks like a guide book, but is no more just that than Meier-Graefe's text is a mere critical survey. Forster arrived in Alexandria in the autumn of 1915 'in a slightly heroic mood'. A Red Cross volunteer, he stuck it for three years, and in that time, 'dressed like a sort of officer', he wrote his guide and came to know the Greek poet C.P. Cavafy. The guide looks into history, layout and buildings, and remarks on points of interest, but Forster's gift was to personify the city. She had memories and a conscience, and unpleasant neighbours such as 'the solid but unattractive figure of Rome'. She was clever, disputatious and tolerant, and then chastened by a millenium of Arab domination. Alexandria's great age was Jewish and Christian, and lasted from 200 B.C. until its conquest by Amr in 641 A.D. Forster delighted in the manipulative skills of its philosophers and theologians, and excused them on grounds that they tried to mediate between God and humanity. Arius, the heretical presbyter at the church of St. Mark in Alexandria, is commended by Forster. Arius, who stressed Christ's youth and humanity, fell foul of Athanasius, and was excommunicated. Forster clearly admired his tendency 'to magnify the human in the divine', and had he met Meier-Graefe in the context of the Old Kingdom they might have found common ground with respect to love, humanity and order in the world.

Forster's Alexandria, especially as recounted in his section *The Spiritual City*, sounds like an ideal city-state beset by troublesome fanatics, followers of a surly and unapproachable Jehovah or Islam's God of power. Inevitably, things turned out badly. Alexandria came to a sort of life again under Mohammed Ali, who came to power after the Napoleonic incursion. (Mohammed Ali, whose name Lane's faithful refused to brand on their camels, belongs to a history of Egypt where nothing is as it first appears; the founder of a Turkish dynasty, he was in fact an Albanian, born at Cavala in Macedonia.) Mohammed Ali developed the city, and then it was bombarded and substantially damaged by a British force in 1882. In Forster's time its prosperity was based on cotton, onions and eggs, and he could see little prospect of any other sort of progress. He concluded his history of the city with a poem by Cavafy addressed to Mark Anthony attending to the omen which heralded his defeat. Cavafy warned against lamenting a vanishing fortune, 'your life's work that has failed, your schemes that have proved illusions'. Cavafy's Mark Anthony might have been Forster himself musing on the old days when Alexandria acknowledged the love of God. He might almost be the model for Meier-Graefe entranced by that ideal of an art both humane and firm. Egypt tantalized, gave rise to dreams and then to disappointments: Forster's bombarded city with its onions, Meier-Graefe's newly plastered Sphinx. The later writers insisted on futility. Where Lane wrote as a man of science who might understand Egypt, Meier-Graefe and Forster are, by contrast, companionable, walking and talking, up against it with nothing on their side which might carry the day against the forces of contemporary darkness. And Loti, who reads like a hunted solitary clinging to the shadows, quite relished his isolation.

Loti and the others dreamed of civilization fled, but Egypt was adaptable, prepared even to stand in for sporting England. In a memoir, *Egyptian Service 1902–1946*, Sir Thomas Russell Pasha apologized in his foreword for 'not mentioning her modern industrialization, her cotton factories, her spinning and weaving works, her electrification plans and other big schemes'. Nor did he mention a single monument. Woburn Abbey was the family home, and 'Little Johnny', the Prime Minister, a recent ancestor. Thomas was an English Adviser and Commandant of the Cairo police from 1917, 'and from 1919 to 1924 had little time to think of anything except political riots and assassinations'. In 1929 he became head of the Central Narcotics Intelligence Bureau, and throughout was involved with 'right-hand men' in 'ticklish situations'.

Egyptian Service is more informative on the life of the place than anything since Lane, largely because the author, who had belonged to the poor sporting set at Cambridge, transferred his interests in ferreting and hunting intact to Egypt. In the desert he met again the countrymen friends of his childhood, although in their African incarnations they were guides and trackers, especially men of the Bisharin tribe of the Hamedorab of the Sudan. He looked into the arcana of desert life, into gazelle hunting and snake charming, and was explicit on drug running and consumption. He belonged to the world of capable managers, not often at a loss. He described an ugly looking demonstration headed by a martyred corpse on a bier. Not entirely satisfied he remembered an unfailing test taught him by an old Austrian police officer during his days in Alexandria. Covertly he applied the tip of a lighted cigarette to the dangling hand of the corpse, with immediate results. *Egyptian Service* was also an adventure story, bizarrely staffed: old Frankel, an Austrian in Alexandria, and perhaps at heart one of a long line of head keepers from the Woburn estate.

Thomas Russell served thirty-two Egyptian Governments in forty-four years, and as Commandant in Cairo took orders from twenty-nine different Ministers of Interior in as many years. Society was undermined by greed, self-indulgence and idleness – and the author spoke his mind about the gilded youth of Cairo. The writer also acknowledged unforeseen consequences, one of the great Egyptian themes. The Egyptian fellahin were subject to bilharzia and ankylostoma, waterborne intestinal parasitic diseases once confined to the northern parts of the Delta. Due to improvements in irrigation, mainly that of the Aswan barrage of 1902, the water table in Upper Egypt had risen sufficiently to sustain the water-snails which carried the debilitating diseases. Russell estimated that Egyptian labour capacity had fallen almost by half as a result, and that the general debility had prompted an epidemic of drug-taking: cocaine from 1916, and heroin a little later. William Golding took up the consequences theme in the 1980s, remarking that Egypt's antiquities were being rotted by rising salt, formerly washed out by the annual inundation.

William Golding's *An Egyptian Journal* fits beautifully into the tradition. It more or less announces itself as a failure, for the author, travelling on the Nile in a malfunctioning cabin-cruiser, can scarcely see anything beyond the river banks, and on those banks only ugly brickworks. Nor can he think of anything conclusive to say, or anything which would match up to his more laudable intentions to range through the -ologies. He had ideas on the mysteries of the East, and one day in Cairo saw an old, jewelled woman narrating in a café to an enthralled group of young men: dirty stories, his dragoman admitted. And then he, and Ann, noticed that women were scarce in the main thoroughfares, but in a majority in the side streets. What did it mean? They had identified an *interface*, but could read its meaning no further than the word, which kept coming back. An interface: *An Egyptian Journal* is another Egyptian book of the Word. 'Malesh' recurs, signifying an acceptance of what fate might have to offer, but at the same time it was a word which engrossed Golding: its sound and meaning, both. 'Sebakh', too, spurred him into an eloquent section on soil, litter, debris . . . and the unearthing of WORDS, on papyrus dumped or hidden in antiquity.

Mallarmé reckoned presence as tedium, and Golding in Egypt might have agreed. The Luxor Museum he thought a 'must', but the visit had clearly taken the edge from his appetite. Oxyrhynchus, on the other hand, was another matter, partly because he never got there, and even had he succeeded there was nothing to see. The name meant 'Sharp-nose' or 'Pike', and was one of the fourteen shrines to Osiris, although with a difference, for all the others held a piece of the body of Osiris cut up by Set, or Typhon. At Oxyrhynchus, though, a pike had swallowed the penis of the god. And then the locals distinguished themselves by dumping scripts with the rubbish. He described a moment in 1897 when a Dr. Hunt, excavating, read in Greek, '.. and then shalt thou see clearly to cast out the mote which is in thy brother's eye' (Matthew, 7.3). It was a moment of origin, of words and phrases coming together, the emergence of meaning. Where words are involved he is a different writer, and words flourish in the absence of the things themselves. The trip to Egypt may have been a necessity in the generation of his text, but in the main it was an occasion to be endured, and the less seen the better. Lane, savouring the names of Egyptian materials, was of the same camp, and Loti, enraptured by chanted readings, would have been sympathetic to the Englishman at Oxyrhynchus. Like his precursors he also relished silence, the ideal ground on which words began to figure; and like them, too, his Egypt was cacophonous with broken bearings and Musak.

Writers' Egypt could be an extravagant place, comparable to Europe, but always different. Photography, more disinterested than writing, takes things as they come and argues for similarities in one world. At the same time, photographers inflect their findings towards some preferred or irresistible model. Paul Strand, at work in Egypt in the 1960s, was touched by an idea of industrialization and five-year planning. Bohm's Egypt, although less ideological than Strand's, also has its secrets. Those cinema posters, for example, torn on a Cairo wall, look more like a homage to European painting in the fifties when torn printing stood for a persistent organic impulse in society. And the polychrome poster of tempting Sozan at Aswan, belongs further back; she might even be a survivor from some thirties programme, when folk art meant creativity in society at large. And that child, too, playing with a toy felucca on the Nile at Aswan might be a successor to those animated children who walk the pages of Kertesz and of Cartier-Bresson in the 1940s and before. A keen critical mind, however, might go into enough historic detail to miss the point. This Egypt of greengrocers, tailors, rope merchants, card-players and other idlers and passers-by lies open to the eye, and looks as if it might be known as well as read: people sit, eat and compose themselves thus. The pictures declare and declare for everyday life, for a kind of life which begins to look surprising in industrialized cultures encapsulated in air-conditioned motors, theme-food restaurants and among fitted kitchens in designer homes. This Egypt is ideological, or biased, in the sense that it recalls earlier days among materials. Those pictures of hand-prints on house walls intended to ward off the evil eye might amount to more than another observation on regional life; rather they might signify touch, contact and the stuff of life, in the face of a visiting culture hermetically sealed and fundamentally out of touch.

Bibliographical Note

LANE, Edward William: *An Account of the Manners and Customs of the Modern Egyptians*, London, 1836.

FLAUBERT, Gustave: *Flaubert in Egypt*, translated and edited by Francis Steegmuller, London, 1972. This book is compiled from the *Oeuvres Complètes*, Notes de Voyages, I, Paris, 1910, and *Les Lettres d'Egypte*, Paris, 1965.

DE NERVAL, Gérard: *Voyage en Orient*, Paris, 1851. It came out in English in two volumes in 1929 as *The Women of Cairo: Scenes of Life in the Orient*, with an introduction by Conrad Elphinstone.

NIGHTINGALE, Florence: *Letters from Egypt: A Journey on the Nile, 1849–50*, London, 1987.

EDWARDS, Amelia B.: *A Thousand Miles up the Nile*, London, 1877. A second edition came out in 1888; it was republished in 1982, with an introduction by Quentin Crewe.

MONTBARD, Georges: *The Land of the Sphinx*, London, 1894.

LOTI, Pierre: *Egypt*, London, 1909.

FORSTER, E.M.: *Alexandria*, London, 1982. The first edition was published in Alexandria in 1922, and the second in 1938; a new American edition appeared in 1961, with a new introduction by the author, and that was the basis for the London edition, with an additional introduction by Lawrence Durrell.

MEIER-GRAEFE, Julius: *Pyramid and Temple*, London, 1931. Translated from the German by Roger Hinks.

RUSSELL, Sir Thomas (Sir Thomas Russell Pasha, K.B.E., C.M.G.): *Egyptian Service, 1902–1946*, London, 1949.

GOLDING, William: *An Egyptian Journal*, London, 1985.

Egypt Illustrated

A bibliographical survey by Ian Jeffrey

Egypt and Nubia. *Two volumes, from drawings made on the spot by David Roberts, R.A., lithographed by Louis Haghe, and with an historical description by William Brockedon, London, 1846.*

Louis Haghe made eighty-five lithographs from Roberts' drawings, and Brockedon accompanied each picture with a page of text. In this most elegant account of Egypt and Nubia, Roberts concentrated on the mosques of Cairo which seem to have been as fascinating in the 1840s as were the pyramids. Roberts illustrated street life, too: a slave market, a coffee-shop, and dancing girls ('ghawazels'): 'The Ghawazels are dancing girls who perform unveiled in the public streets to amuse the rabble; their dances have little elegance and less decorum.' Roberts was the first, and almost the last, illustrator of Egypt to look at folk and street life. Brockedon wrote like a grandee. Roberts drew the Holy Tree at Metereah, under which the Holy Family had rested on their flight into Egypt, and Brockedon added: 'Devotees, however, have not been deterred by its holiness from cutting their names and initials on every available spot on its withered trunk.' Roberts approved of the Nubians, 'wild people' who were 'brave, generous and confiding', and as servants 'the most faithful that can be obtained in the valley of the Nile'. The artist's street scenes swarm with people, over and against a dignified, remote text. With the coming of photography, however, that relationship changes; the pictures themselves become staid, and texts both garrulous and irreverent – among English photographers, at least.

Egypte et Nubie: Sites et Monuments les plus intéressants pour l'étude de l'art et de l'histoire. *Photographs by Félix Teynard, ingénieur civil, Paris, 1858.*

Teynard's 160 plates came out in thirty-two books, one per week, and amount to one of the most beautiful, though least known, surveys of Egypt. Like Roberts, he was interested in the mosques of Cairo although resolute, too, in his attention to pyramids and temples. The people scarcely feature in his delicate studies of architecture, softly done in calotype. Teynard was a materialist who registered the fall of sunlight on stone, and the pictures are rich in shadows and silhouettes. If there were none suitable they might be contrived by, for example, propping a walking stick against a temple wall, as he did at Beni Hassan. Teynard's Egypt looks convincing, unedited; graffiti disfigure temple walls, and stones seem to spew out of the flanks of the Cheops Pyramid at Giza. Teynard was at his best with carvings in low relief where his taste for refined shadow in light could be indulged. He was a taciturn commentator who noticed, for instance, that although the Sphinx was turned towards the rising sun it was not exactly aligned. His Egypt told a story of grandeur and decline; everything before the age of Alexander the Great was grandiose and ornamented in a way which was in keeping, and after that *belle époque* it was downhill all the way into the ephemeral constructions and barbarities of the Christian age. His pictures of the major pyramids have never been approached, let alone equalled.

Cairo, Sinai & Jerusalem. *A series of sixty photographic views by Francis Frith, with descriptions by Mrs Poole and Reginald Stuart Poole, London, 1860.*

Egypt, Sinai & Jerusalem. *A series of twenty photographic views by Francis Frith, with descriptions by Mrs Poole and Reginald Stuart Poole, London, 1860.*

Egypt and Palestine. *Photographs and description by Francis Frith, London, 1862.*

Egypt, Nubia & Ethiopia. *One hundred stereoscopic photographs taken by Francis Frith for Messrs. Negretti and Zambra, with descriptions and numerous wood engravings by Joseph Bonomi, author of* **Nineveh and its Palaces,** *and notes by Samuel Sharpe, author of* **The History of Egypt,** *London, 1862.*

Francis Frith made the most of Egypt and of the East. His first books were the outcome of a journey of 1857, and he returned in 1859–60. Like David Roberts, he looked at the mosques of Cairo and photographed some deserted street scenes. Frith had nothing of the finesse of Teynard who was able to make beautiful abstracts from a pyramid, palm trees and a standing figure. But Frith's pictures may never have been meant to draw attention to themselves. They seem, instead, to function as occasions for writing, and writing, moreover, which reads as speech. The Pooles filled Frith's tranquil city with the cries of victims. They pointed out execution sites, and went into detail on a blood-stained history. In front of a street view they recounted bastinading and beheading by the Walee, ruffianly police lately discontinued; and they told the story of Mehemet Ali's treacherous massacre of the Mameluks in 1811 with Ibrahim Pasha, a sort of Prince Regent, running to and fro on the roof of the Arsenal screaming with delight. In the second place, Egypt was the site of many a biblical event which could be brought vividly to life in the presence of Frith's photographs. Bonomi and Sharpe presuppose the most acute attention to details, to be read from the pictures via stereoscopes.

Frith himself refrained until **Egypt and Palestine** (1862), which became his story of the trials suffered by a photographer: 'When (at the Second Cataract, one thousand miles from the mouth of the Nile, with the thermometer at 110° in my tent) the collodion actually boiled upon the glass plate.' At the same spot he met one of the most exuberant characters in the whole of photography history, the Brandy Sheikh, a victim to English brandy, which he drank neat as a preliminary to guiding boats through the rapids: 'The Brandy Sheikh roared more hoarsely than ever; he trembled with sham excitement; he grasped a big stick, and belaboured the men who worked best with a relentless idiocy; he threw himself into the water, swam wildly about, scrambled on board again, and demanded more brandy, or he could not work in the water.' Frith, up to his neck in spectacular trouble, is a far cry from Teynard charting the rise and fall of civilizations. Describing the ruins, Frith insisted on translations as though he would have Amon, in the Great Hall at Karnak, speak to Seti I in his own voice: 'I grant thee my domain . . . . . . and the Nubians also shall be the footstool beneath thy sandals.' Frith's photographs opened a door to a hubbub to which he, Amon and The Brandy Sheikh were pungent contributors. Photography has always stimulated explication and reminiscence, and Frith was one of the first to capitalize on that potential.

Egypt: Architecture, Landscape, Life of the People. *Photographs by Ludwig Borchardt and Herbert Ricke, Orbis Terrarum, Germany. Borchardt dated his introduction, Cairo, July 1929.*

The Orbis Terrarum surveys were comprehensive, and finely printed in Germany. Ricke, who made most of the photographs here, worked comparatively, showing the Sphinx, for instance, in relation to surrounding pyramids, and from enough angles to allow it to be properly gauged. The Orbis Terrarum photographers were working in an age interested in map-making and in resource charts and this is reflected here in aerial photographs of prime sites. **Egypt** holds 272 pictures captioned in four languages, although without any more explanatory text. Enough could be remarked from the wealth of material on show, in geological, anthropological and archaeological terms. Something of the Orbis Terrarum spirit survives in Paul Strand's **Living Egypt** (1969), though made more familiar and garrulous.

Egypt. *Photographs by Hoyningen-Huene, with text by George Steindorff, New York, 1943; a second, revised edition was published in 1945.*

Hoyningen-Huene, a celebrated fashion photographer, discovered a most stylish Egypt, much of it in New York at the Metropolitan Museum of Art, and in the Museum of Fine Arts, Boston. More even than the fastidious Félix Teynard, a century before, he loved the shadows of Egypt, and one of his most striking pictures is of the shadow of the Pyramid of Khufu at Giza bringing order to the village of Kafr-el-Samman. The whole, with its colossal statues parading in front of curtain walls and its sharp highlighting with deep shadows, looks like a theatrical spectacle played by elegant marionettes in gold, granite and limestone. This is the most courtly of Egyptian projects, and one which emphasized precious materials and fine workmanship rather than the rough voice of Amon and the crushing of the Nubians.

L'Egypte face à face. *Photographs by Etienne Sved, with a text by Tristan Tzara, Lausanne, 1954.*

Tzara and his photographer found ancient life replicated in the streets of Cairo and, more especially, in the villages of Egypt. Sved found up-to-date versions of the kind of daily life recorded in old reliefs and paintings, as if an essential folk-life endured. In Tzara's introduction the old artefacts appear as an exemplary synthesis drawn from life, with photography showing their present relevance. Tzara thought that one advantage of this book was to clarify connections between art and life, and to warn against gratuitousness in art. Julius Meier-Graefe and other humanist writers of the 1930s would have recognized Sved's project and Tzara's forceful apologia.

Sun, Stones and Silence. *Photographs by Dorothy Hales Gray, with an introduction by Georges Duhamel and text by Robert Payne, New York, 1963.*

This photographer presupposes an interested audience able to assess, for example, the façade of Abu Simbel from different points of view. At the same time, and in passing, guides and guards and odd passers-by crop up as signs of an irremediable local life: a snake charmer shows off his stock-in-trade, and a donkey-man holds still for a moment or two. Photographers would never again be so candid about just being there in passing.

Living Egypt. *Photographs by Paul Strand, with a text by James Aldridge, London, 1969.*

Paul Strand was unenthusiastic about Ancient Egypt, and scarcely allowed it into this survey of 105 pictures. 'The long and painful sleep may finally be over', were James Aldridge's last words. Strand's Egypt was peopled by handsome folk seen in close-up, posing for their pictures, as they might have done for a local cameraman. Kindred faces reappear in Duane Michals' **Merveilles d'Egypte**, taken by an Aswan portraitist. Strand, committed to the contemporary people of Egypt, concentrated on their skills as traders, artisans and folk artists. His own pictures are often made up of architectural planes almost parallel to the picture surface, and separated and distinguished by bands of shadow. Where Frith's Egypt drew on the Bible and on stories from the **Thousand and One Nights**, Strand's was an arrangement to be gauged by an artist or craftsman with an eye for point, line and plane. Strand was acting on behalf of the people, against an enervating weight in tradition. Dorothy Bohm, who works over much of the same terrain, is less pious; her people are more prone to improvise, to enjoy leisure and luxury; and they put up with the past and with the tourism which it generates.

Merveilles d'Egypte. *Photographs by Duane Michals, Paris, 1978.*

Michals begins at Abu Simbel holding a strip of paper marking the moment of his arrival there: 3.52 p.m., 1 February 1978. Eighty pictures on he appears bowing towards the stepped temple at Sakkara and throwing a fine, deep shadow on the desert. At one point, over a series of six pictures, he appears building his own rough stone pyramid at Giza; and over five frames a guardian confronts him with a gun at Luxor, the result of the photographer's taste for early morning visits to sites. He also made pictures of the pyramids by moonlight which, in a note, he remembers as one of the most beautiful and romantic experiences of his life. Michals looks like a successor to Frith; if only Frith had done more about the Brandy Sheikh and those hunts for red-legged partridges. Michals' preoccupations are with the here-and-now of travelling, with accidents, chance meetings and with the feelings aroused by the great sites: in one set of six he sets fire to a newspaper spread on an altar at Luxor, with Amon and the rest not looking on. Both Egypt and Michals come enhanced out of the meeting.

Egypte. *Photographs by Bernard Plossu, with a text by Carole Naggar, Paris, 1979.*

This set of thirty-four pictures might have been meant to complement William Golding's **Egyptian Journal** (1985) for it features what caught Plossu's eye – with history well over the horizon. He travelled on the Nile, but remarked on a boatman punting, on the splash of a blade in the water and on a bellied sail with tassels. And humanity caught his eye too: suave gestures or the fall of a robe. 'I saw this', the pictures remark, as if the commonplace were remarkable. It may be the land of the pyramids and of the Aswan High Dam, but for this photographer there is nothing more beautiful than mist on a morning road and oil stains in the wet. Plossu tests the perceptive power of his audience, and its refinement, just as Michals stimulates good humour and sympathy.

December morning on the
Nile, Cairo.